ROBERT
MAASS

A

is

for

Autumn

Christy Ottaviano Books

HENRY HOLT AND COMPANY · NEW YORK

For Carroll,
who makes every autumn
more colorful.

A

is

for

Autumn

and

Apples,

of

course.

B

is

for

Birds

that

fly

south

to

warmer

winter

homes.

C

is

for

Colors

as

leaves

begin

to

change.

D

is

for

Daylight,

getting

shorter

as

the

weather

gets

colder.

E

is

for

Exercise.

You

can

never

get

too

much

of

it.

F

is

for

Frost,

when

dew

freezes

and

water

turns

to

ice.

G

is

for

Games.

Running

hard

keeps

away

the

chills.

H

is

for

Halloween.

Bring

out

the

spooky

costumes!

I

is

for

Ice

Cream,

which

is

delicious

in

any

season.

J

is

for

Jacket.

It's

getting

chilly!

K

is

for

Kayak,

taking

one

last

paddle

for

the

season.

L

is

for

Leaves

littering

the

ground

with

vibrant

color.

M

is

for

Monarch

butterfly

gathering

nectar

before

the

long

migration

home.

N

is

for

Neighborhood.

It's

where

we

live.

O

is

for

Owl,

a

bird

of

the

night.

P

is

for

Pumpkins.

They

come

in

lots

of

shapes

and

colors.

Q

is

for

Quilt,

for

that

extra

layer

of

warmth.

R

is

for

Rake.

Time

to

gather

fallen

leaves

before

snow

comes.

S

is

for

Scarecrow

stuffed

with

corn

husks

and

standing

tall.

T

is

for

Thanksgiving

when

families

and

friends

share

a

special

meal.

U

is

for

Umbrella,

keeping

us

dry

in

the

cool

autumn

rain.

V

is

for

Vegetables

like

gourds

and

squash.

W

is

for

Wood

burning

in

fireplaces

to

keep

us

warm.

X

is

for

Train

Crossing,

letting

us

know

when

trains

are

near.

Y

is

for

Yellow

as

bright

as

afternoon

sunshine.

Z

is

for

Zipper.

Zip

up,

winter's

on

its

way!

Henry Holt and Company, LLC
Publishers since 1866
175 Fifth Avenue
New York, New York 10010
mackids.com

Library of Congress
Cataloging-in-Publication Data
Maass, Robert.
A is for autumn / by Robert Maass.
— 1st ed.
p. cm.
"Christy Ottaviano books."
Summary: Photographs and
simple text present a variety
of things seen in the fall.
ISBN 978-0-8050-9093-2
[1. Autumn—Fiction. 2. Alphabet.]
I. Title.
PZ7.M11158Aae 2011
[E]—dc22
2010040333

First Edition—2011
Designed by April Ward

Printed in May 2011 in China by
South China Printing Company Ltd.,
Dongguan City, Guangdong Province

1 3 5 7 9 10 8 6 4 2